THE 10

Most Wondrous Ancient Sites

Carol Drake

Series Editor
Jeffrey D. Wilhelm

Much thought, debate, and research went into choosing and ranking the 10 items in each book in this series. We realize that everyone has his or her own opinion of what is most significant, revolutionary, amazing, deadly, and so on. As you read, you may agree with our choices, or you may be surprised — and that's the way it should be!

Franklin Watts®

an imprint of

SCHOLASTIC

www.scholastic.com/librarypublishing

A Rubicon book published in association with Scholastic Inc.

Rubicon © 2007 Rubicon Publishing Inc.
www.rubiconpublishing.com

Associate Publishers: Kim Koh, Miriam Bardswich
Project Editor: Amy Land
Editor: Christine Boocock
Creative Director: Jennifer Drew
Senior Designer: Jeanette MacLean
Graphic Designer: Doug Baines

The publisher gratefully acknowledges the following for permission to reprint copyrighted material in this book.

Every reasonable effort has been made to trace the owners of copyrighted material and to make due acknowledgment. Any errors or omissions drawn to our attention will be gladly rectified in future editions.

Cover: The Great Pyramid and Sphinx–Shutterstock

Library and Archives Canada Cataloguing in Publication

Drake, Carol
        The 10 most wondrous ancient sites/Carol Drake.

Includes index.
ISBN 978-1-55448-467-6

        1. Readers (Elementary) 2. Readers—Curiosities and wonders.
I. Title. II. Title: Ten most wondrous ancient sites.

PE1117.D734 2007   428.6   C2007-900547-0

5 6 7 8 9 10 11 12 13 14   10   20 19 18 17 16 15 14 13 12 11

Printed in Singapore

Contents

PACK YOUR BAGS!

PERU

ROME

EGYPT

If you had to plan a vacation, where would you go? Would you choose a beach resort, an adventure travel experience, or a trip to an ancient site? If you did not say yes to the last choice, you might be surprised to learn what you are missing. Ancient sites often date back hundreds, if not thousands, of years. They can inform us about history, different cultures, and far-off places.

Ancient doesn't have to mean stuffy or boring. The sites on our list are exciting enough to attract lots of tourists, both young and old. Some of these sites are remote and it's an adventure just to get there. Others sit right in the middle of modern cities, where eager tourists have to fight traffic and crowds of people. Whatever it takes, it's all worth it. Visiting these destinations helps us to understand ancient civilizations and cultures.

To rank our list of the 10 most wondrous ancient sites, we looked at the age of each site. We also noted the beauty of the design and the complexity of the construction. Finally, we considered the historical significance of each site and its enduring appeal.

Join us on an adventure through time and across the globe. Explore our 10 most wondrous ancient sites!

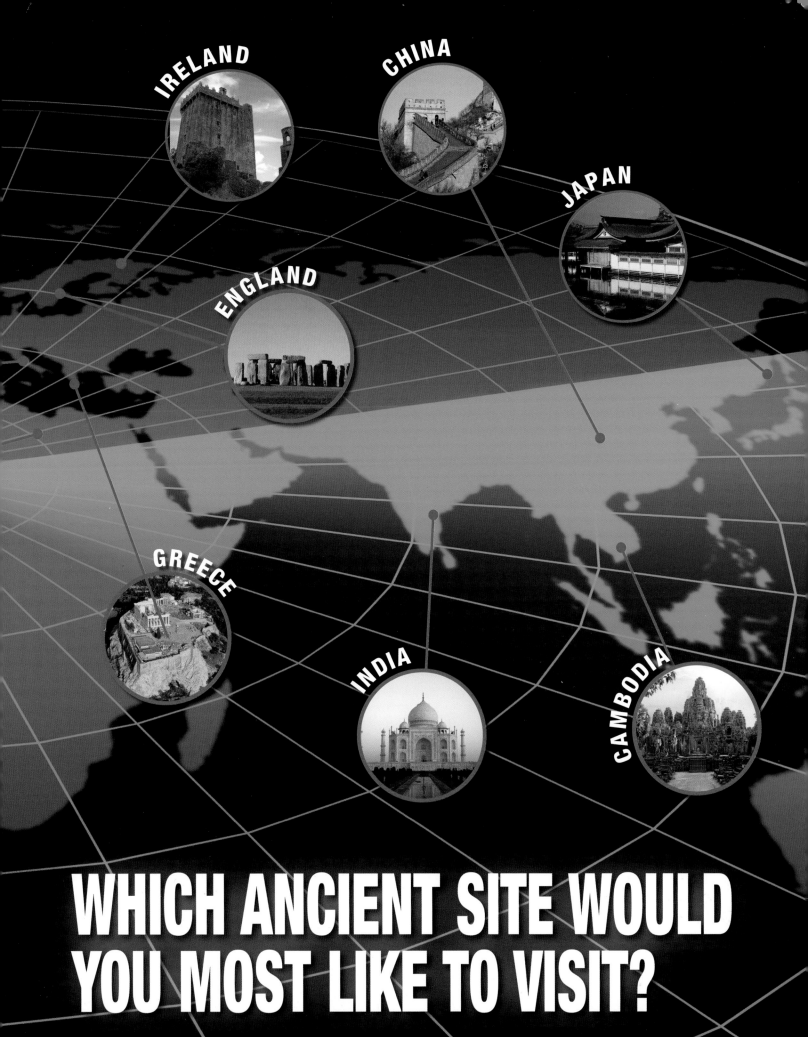

IRELAND

CHINA

JAPAN

ENGLAND

GREECE

INDIA

CAMBODIA

WHICH ANCIENT SITE WOULD YOU MOST LIKE TO VISIT?

Blarney Castle has been rebuilt twice since the 10th century — the current structure has been standing since 1446 A.D.!

WHAT IS IT? Built in 1446 A.D., this ancient castle is home to the world-famous Blarney Stone.

WHERE IS IT? Blarney Village, near County Cork on the south coast of Ireland

WHY IT'S FABULOUS: Hope you aren't afraid of germs. Every year thousands of tourists kiss the Blarney Stone hoping for a special gift.

You may not know it, but you've probably heard blarney in action. People with this "gift of the gab" are great at using blarney to talk their way out of any situation. For people who weren't born with this gift, there's an easy way to get it – just kiss the Blarney Stone!

The Blarney Stone is one of Ireland's most famous landmarks. Kissing it is said to give you the ability to always know the right thing to say. You can find this magical rock wedged into one of the walls in the 600-year-old Blarney Castle. However, you really have to want the "gift of the gab" because, like most good fortune, you have to work a bit to get it.

First, you climb a spiral staircase up three levels. Then you go up an extremely steep and narrow staircase to reach the top of the tower. The stone can only be reached by lying flat on your back and hanging upside down. Remember, you are about five stories above ground! You then grab the vertical bars and the keeper of the stone holds onto you as you dangle there to plant your kiss. Scary!

Those who tell you they weren't nervous when they did it are probably full of blarney!

blarney: *smooth and flattering talk; nonsense*

Find out about another castle that is a tourist attraction. Compare it to Blarney Castle. Which would you recommend as a place to see? Why?

ORIGINS

Blarney Castle has been rebuilt twice. The original 10th century wooden castle was replaced by a stone structure in 1210. This stone structure was owned by smooth talker Cormac McCarthy, King of Munster, Ireland's biggest province. In 1314, McCarthy was given the Blarney Stone by the king of Scotland, Robert the Bruce, as thanks for support in battle. McCarthy had supplied Bruce with troops to help him win the Battle of Bannockburn, against the English. In 1446, a third castle replaced the stone structure. This structure has one of the biggest rectangular-shaped towers on any castle in Ireland. The castle is L-shaped and parts of the walls are 12 feet thick! The Blarney Stone was built into one of these walls.

 Why does history add interest and significance to a site?

DETAILS

Blarney Castle sits on top of a maze of eerie passageways and caves. In 1646, when the castle was under attack from the English, everyone fled to safety through these tunnels and caves. Today, those who brave the narrow entryway and darkness will find the castle's prison and damp dungeon! More pathways lead visitors through the gardens and to the witch stone. This stone, shaped like a witch's head, is said to imprison a witch who comes out at night! This witch is supposed to be the same one who first told McCarthy about the Blarney Stone's powers.

This ancient site is linked to legends, like the one about the witch. What makes legends fascinating? What is your favorite legend?

HUMAN CONNECTION

In 1646, Oliver Cromwell, an army colonel, worked with English forces to take control of Ireland. He ordered his men to drive the McCarthys from their castle, but they eventually returned. In 1690, the Battle of the Boyne took place. This battle was between Protestant and Catholic forces fighting for the English throne and for religious power in Ireland. After the battle, the McCarthys were forced out of Blarney Castle for good. Legend has it that the McCarthys threw their gold into a nearby lake before leaving. One unlucky owner spent a fortune draining the lake. Instead of gold, all he found was that the story was a bit of blarney! In 1703, Sir James Jefferyes bought the castle. He was the governor of Cork City. His relatives still own the castle today.

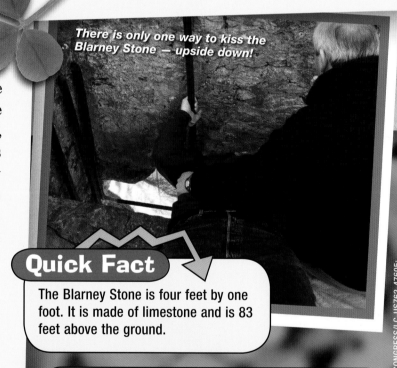

There is only one way to kiss the Blarney Stone — upside down!

Quick Fact

The Blarney Stone is four feet by one foot. It is made of limestone and is 83 feet above the ground.

The Expert Says...

"Reportedly, Queen Elizabeth I (1533-1603) coined the term 'blarney' during the lengthy, tiresome negotiations concerning control of the [castle]."

— Dr. Joe Nickell, author

10 9 8 7 6

REASONS FOR VISITING BLARNEY CASTLE

Read this list and plan ahead!

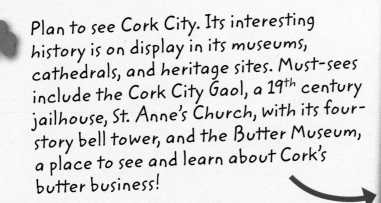 Plan to see Cork City. Its interesting history is on display in its museums, cathedrals, and heritage sites. Must-sees include the Cork City Gaol, a 19th century jailhouse, St. Anne's Church, with its four-story bell tower, and the Butter Museum, a place to see and learn about Cork's butter business!

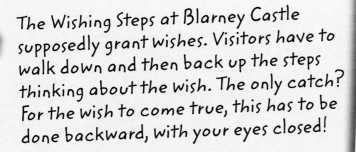 The Wishing Steps at Blarney Castle supposedly grant wishes. Visitors have to walk down and then back up the steps thinking about the wish. The only catch? For the wish to come true, this has to be done backward, with your eyes closed!

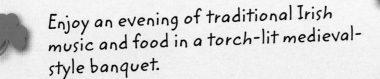 Enjoy an evening of traditional Irish music and food in a torch-lit medieval-style banquet.

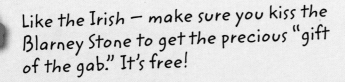 Like the Irish — make sure you kiss the Blarney Stone to get the precious "gift of the gab." It's free!

Bring your camera. The castle is set in incredible surroundings — village, lake, and countryside.

Cork City has a population of 123,000, making it the second-largest city in Ireland.

Take Note

Blarney Castle is #10 on our list. It captures the character of its country and citizens. What makes it unique is the wall with its famous rock!

- Do you think that we're "full of blarney" for having put Blarney Castle on our list? Would you have done the same and why?

5 4 3 2 1

Itsukushima isn't the only Shinto shrine in Japan. There are about 90,000 in all! Some say this religion, Shinto, goes as far back as 500 B.C.

SHRINE

Open any travel book about Japan and you're likely to see pictures of sushi, Mount Fuji, and pagodas. You might also find pictures of the famous Otorii (oh-toh-ree) Gate. This beautiful gate is an important symbol of Japan. It guards the entrance to the ancient Itsukushima (it-soo-koo-she-mah) Shinto shrine, which dates back to the 6th century A.D. According to legend, three sea goddesses chose the sacred site. The shrine was built in their honor. Given the shrine's spectacular setting and mountain background, we think those goddesses had good taste!

Itsukushima shrine almost met with tragedy on August 6, 1945, the day an atomic bomb was dropped on Hiroshima. The shrine is a 15-minute ferry ride away from Hiroshima. It was miraculously spared from the bomb.

In 1996, the shrine was declared a UNESCO World Heritage Site. This means that it is an important cultural site that UNESCO will protect and preserve.

pagodas: *Asian temples*
UNESCO: *United Nations Educational, Scientific and Cultural Organization*

ITSUKUSHIMA SHRINE

ORIGINS

Many Japanese people used to believe that Miyajima Island, where Itsukushima stands, was a holy place. They even built the shrine on stilts in the sea because they didn't want to disturb the sacred land! The first shrine was built in 593 A.D., by a man called Saeki Kuramoto (say-ay-kee koo-rah-mo-to). In 1168, new buildings and the Otorii gate were built.

DETAILS

There are 56 buildings in the shrine. The Otorii, or gate, is made of camphor, a type of wood. It is painted red and stands about 52 feet tall. Some of the other buildings include the main sanctuary, an outdoor stage, a high stage, and a drama stage. The shrine has curved lines, diamond-shaped lattices, and thatched cypress roofs. The buildings are connected by covered passageways. Over centuries, Itsukushima has been damaged by fires and typhoons. It has been restored by workers skilled in ancient crafts. Since it was built in 1168, the Otorii gate alone has been reconstructed 17 times!

high stage: *elevated stage used for traditional Japanese performances*
lattices: *crossed strips, arranged to form a diagonal pattern of open spaces between the strips*

? The shrine has been preserved using traditional methods even though it would be easier to fix using modern technology. In general, how does using ancient methods help to preserve the past?

HUMAN CONNECTION

The original shrine was built during the reign of Empress Suiko (soo-ee-koh). She ruled from 592 to 628 A.D. She was the first woman and 33rd emperor to rule Japan. Itsukushima is an important Shinto shrine. In the Shinto religion, people worship nature. Miyajima Island has been revered for thousands of years because of its forests, wildlife, and Mount Misen. The highest place on the island, rising more than 1,700 feet, Mount Misen is an impressive natural site. This makes it important to people who practice Shinto.

? A major part of the Japanese culture is a belief in the importance of beauty. How is Itsukushima an example of this?

Quick Fact

To keep the site pure, visitors to Itsukushima are ordered to obey three rules: No cutting down trees; no giving birth; and no dying!

SEA OF JAPAN

ITSUKUSHIMA SHRINE

Japan

TOKYO

HAIKU HOMAGE

One of Japan's most famous art forms is haiku poetry. Learn all about it in this article.

An old silent pond
A frog leaps into the pond,
splash! Silence again.

— Matsuo Basho

This is the Otorii, or gate, that leads to Itsukushima shrine.

This famous Japanese haiku was written by Matsuo Basho in the 1600s. Matsuo was a samurai poet who perfected the haiku, a poem written with three lines of five, seven, and five syllables.

As the son of a samurai, Matsuo was going to follow in his father's footsteps. He trained to be a warrior but when his lord, or sponsor, died in 1666, Matsuo became a full-time poet. Matsuo made haiku into a respected and important form of artistic expression.

It is said that the poet was inspired by the natural setting around the Itsukushima shrine. Poetry readings and cultural performances still take place at the shrine.

Quick Fact

Visitors can take a cable car or hike up Mount Misen. Many visitors have tea from a giant pot kept in a temple at the top of the mountain. People believe the coals under the pot have burned for 1,200 years! Originally used by Buddhist saint Kobo Daishi (ko-boh day-ee-she), the pot is said to have healing powers.

Take Note

Itsukushima is located in a beautiful natural setting. It is a work of art of incomparable physical beauty. As a symbol of its country, and for its age, intricate architecture, and awesome beauty, the shrine ranks higher than Blarney Castle as a fabulous site.
- If you were to recommend Itsukushima as a World Heritage Site, how would you describe it? List all the qualities that you think convinced UNESCO to preserve it for the world to enjoy.

The Expert Says...

" One of the most beautiful and important islands in Japanese mythology [is] Miyajima … The view from Itsukushima [is one of] the three most scenic views in Japan. "

— Jessie Szalay, travel writer

5   4   3   2   1

The wooden floor of the Colosseum was originally covered in sand to soak up the blood of gladiators and others who died there.

WHAT IS IT? An amphitheater, originally built for sporting events and gladiator battles

WHERE IS IT? Rome, Italy

WHY IT'S FABULOUS: The Colosseum is an architectural masterpiece that represents the glory of Rome.

From baseball to boxing, Olympics to concerts, it is hard not to get wrapped up in the excitement of thousands of screaming fans. Modern stadium events aren't as bloody as they were in ancient Rome. But, the idea of 50,000 people gathering to be entertained is not a new one.

In 70 A.D., Emperor Vespasian (ves-pay-see-ahn) needed to do something amazing to win his people's support. What better way than to build a magnificent amphitheater? This amazing structure took around 10 years to build and could seat over 50,000 spectators. The Colosseum was built in a valley. Because of streams that flowed into the valley, drains were first built under the ground to remove water. Then, concrete foundations were laid. The main design was similar to that of other amphitheaters of the time, but this one was bigger than them all! The Colosseum was home to many sporting events and spectacles, including the famous gladiator battles.

Almost 2,000 years after the first stone was laid, this amphitheater is still one of the most famous buildings in the world. It is an architectural masterpiece and a model of engineering effectiveness. Next time you go to a stadium to watch your favorite sport, take a look around. Most modern arenas still follow design principles used to build the Colosseum.

---

amphitheater: *oval or round building with tiers of seats around a central open area*

THE COLOSSEUM

ORIGINS

Ten years after Vespasian started the Colosseum, it was completed. By this time his son Titus was emperor. To celebrate the opening of the Colosseum, parties were held for 100 days! These festivities included violent sports such as fights between gladiators and wild animals.

? Ancient Rome was a very advanced society, known for its buildings and engineering as well as for its culture and arts. Judging from the sports they liked, what else can you conclude about their society?

Quick Fact

During the Middle Ages, most of the marble from the stadium was removed. It was used in the building of palaces and of St. Peter's Basilica. It wasn't until 1749 that Pope Benedict XIV stopped people from taking pieces of the Colosseum.

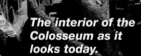

The interior of the Colosseum as it looks today.

DETAILS

Two major earthquakes and a huge fire in 217 A.D. caused severe damage to the amphitheater. Originally, the building covered more than 7.5 acres and had 80 entrance arches. When first built, the Colosseum had no basement. The floor could be flooded to reenact famous naval battles! Domitian, Titus's brother, who ruled from 81 to 89 A.D., built a basement under the structure. Fierce exotic animals were kept underground in this series of pathways and pens. The arena also had four levels of seating. The emperor had his own cushy box seat on the first level with the Roman senators. Some of their names are still visible in the stone. The second level was for nobles, the third for wealthy citizens, and the top level was for the working class.

HUMAN CONNECTION

The Colosseum was used mainly for fights between gladiators. These trained professionals, who were often slaves, fought to the death. Prisoners were also forced to fight with each other or with wild animals imported from Africa and Asia. In 337 A.D., Emperor Constantine made Christianity the official state religion of Rome. In 404 A.D., Emperor Honorarius banned all gladiator games. This form of entertainment was too violent for the Christian church.

reenact: *perform again; go through*

The Expert Says...

"[The Colosseum] stands as a glorious but troubling monument to Roman imperial power and cruelty. Inside it … [The Romans] cold-bloodedly killed literally thousands of people."

— Keith Hopkins, ancient history professor, University of Cambridge

10   9   8   7   6

Some Things NEVER CHANGE

The Colosseum has become the model for most modern stadiums built around the world. It turns out that Vespasian didn't leave much room for improvement. Stadiums are still built using the same circular design as the Colosseum, complete with ascending seats and multiple gates. Do a little research and take a look at the proposed plans for the new New York Yankee Stadium to be completed in 2009. Do the arched windows remind you of those found on the Colosseum? Some things never change. Check out this fact chart :

The Georgia Dome

Stadium	COLOSSEUM Rome, Italy	METRODOME Minneapolis, Minnesota	GEORGIA DOME Atlanta, Georgia
Capacity	55,000	64,000	71,149
Shape	elliptical	rectangular oval	elliptical
Roof	canvas	inflated fabric	cable-supported fabric dome
Floor	sand	artificial turf	artificial turf
Height	157 feet	195 feet	290 feet

A reenactment of two gladiators in battle

Quick Fact

Thousands of wild animals were killed in the Colosseum. Some people believe that the Romans caused the extinction of elephants, hippopotamuses, and lions in certain parts of the world.

Take Note

The Colosseum sits in the heart of Rome, one of the world's busiest modern cities. This amphitheater isn't sacred like Itsukushima. It is much older, though, and for its historical and cultural significance, it ranks higher than the Japanese shrine.
• How does the Colosseum compare with the Itsukushima shrine in structure?

5   3   2   1

(7) MACHU PICCHU

Machu Picchu had over 100 flights of huge stone steps, interconnected water fountains, and drainage and irrigation systems. Crops were grown on terraces, or platforms, carved into the mountainside.

MACHU PICCHU–SHUTTERSTOCK

WHAT IS IT? An ancient Incan city built around 1440 A.D.

WHERE IS IT? The city of Machu Picchu (ma-choo pee-choo) sits at an elevation of almost 8,200 feet in the Andes Mountains of Peru.

WHY IT'S FABULOUS: This Lost City of the Incas gives us an intimate look into their ancient society. It has been called "the eighth wonder of the world."

Indiana Jones showed us that archeologists can be adventuresome movie heroes, but Hiram Bingham was the real thing!

The son of poor missionaries, Bingham became a Yale University professor and married the heiress to the Tiffany jewelry fortune. This fortune allowed him to follow his dreams and take an archeological trip to South America.

With his team resting in camp, Bingham decided to go off on his own with a local farmer. He'd heard a rumor that there were stone walls on a remote ridgetop. It wasn't an easy trip. They made a dangerous river crossing and a tough climb up a densely jungled mountain ridge 1,475 feet above the Urubamba River.

Imagine how he felt on July 24, 1911, when he stumbled upon an ancient village that had existed unknown to the outside world for over 400 years!

Today, approximately 400,000 adventurers trek to Machu Picchu each year. The unsurpassed beauty of both the site and its setting makes it well worth the exotic trip — all good reasons for a #7 ranking.

---

missionaries: *people sent by a church into an area to promote religion and do charitable work*
heiress: *woman who inherits considerable wealth*

MACHU PICCHU

ORIGINS

The Incas were a very powerful people who ruled parts of South America from the 13th to the 16th centuries. Most experts believe that Machu Picchu was built by Pachacutec (pah-cha-coo-teck) who ruled the Incan Empire from 1438 to 1471. Why the city was built remains a mystery! It might have been a finishing school for brides-in-training. (Bingham found mostly female skeletons at the site.) Or it might have been a grand palace for Pachacutec himself.

DETAILS

An ancient, winding road takes tourists to the Sun Gate, the entrance to Machu Picchu. The city includes a guardhouse, a jail, a mausoleum (maw-suh-lee-um), temples, and houses. There are three districts: Sacred, Noble, and Popular. The Sacred district has two temples and a sacred rock that was used to show the precise location of the sun at certain times of the year. This was important to the Incas, who worshipped the Sun God. The Noble district was for the wealthy and priests. The Popular district was for commoners.

mausoleum: *large tomb*

 Archeologists examine ruins to study how people lived in ancient times. Why do you think it is important to learn about ancient civilizations?

An Incan sculpture

HUMAN CONNECTION

In 1532, the Incan Empire was defeated by a Spanish army led by Francisco Pizarro. The Incas lost their riches and their land. Spanish conquerors took their gold and destroyed many historically significant artifacts. But, because it was hidden high up in a mountain, they never found Machu Picchu. The site remained untouched for centuries.

In 1983, UNESCO declared this archeological treasure a World Heritage Site. Unfortunately, the mystery, breathtaking location, and beauty of the site have attracted too many tourists. Pollution, erosion, and landslides threaten to destroy Machu Picchu.

artifacts: *objects produced by humans, especially tools, weapons, or ornaments, of archeological or historical interest*

? Do you think that tourism should be banned or restricted at World Heritage Sites? Explain your position.

Quick Fact

The walls at Machu Picchu were built out of granite rocks. Many of these were carved directly into the mountain face without the use of cement. Yet the stone blocks fit together so smoothly and exactly that even the narrow blade of a knife cannot be inserted between them!

The Expert Says...

" The Inca residential complex of Machu Picchu was, and is, an incredible feat of architecture, sited three thousand feet above the Urubamba River. "

— K. Kris Hirst, archeologist and author

ENTER WITH REVERENCE

Imagine Hiram Bingham's reaction when he hacked his way out of the jungle to discover this "crown jewel in the clouds."

Read Bingham's personal account of what he saw at Machu Picchu, written before he died in 1956 …

After being an explorer, Hiram Bingham served two terms as a U.S. senator from Connecticut.

"In the variety of its charms and the power of its spell, I know of no place in the world which can compare with it. Not only has it great snow peaks looming above the clouds more than two miles overhead, gigantic precipices of many-colored granite rising sheer for [hundreds of miles] above the foamy, glistening, roaring rapids; it has also, in striking contrast, orchids and tree ferns, the delectable beauty of luxurious vegetation, and the mysterious witchery of the jungle."

precipices: *steep, rocky cliffs*
delectable: *delightful; highly pleasing; enjoyable*
luxurious: *present in great abundance; rich*

Quick Fact

Bingham was charming enough to convince Peruvians to let him remove about 5,000 artifacts from the site. The artifacts are in the possession of Yale University, where Bingham worked. Recently, the government of Peru asked for the artifacts back, but Yale has not returned them.

 Do you think Yale should give the artifacts back? Why or why not?

Take Note

Machu Picchu is incredibly beautiful, is located in a spectacular natural setting, and has a fascinating history. Its exciting discovery in the 20th century has taught us much about Incan traditions and lifestyle. This ancient wonder easily made its way to the 7th spot on our list of wondrous sites.

• The Incas and the Romans had many things in common. Both ruled large empires and made important contributions to modern building as well as road and city design. Research these empires. In what ways were they similar or different?

5   4   3   2   1

6 ANGKOR WAT

The central tower of the temple has a distinctive shape said to be that of a lotus bud.

ANGKOR WAT—SHUTTERSTOCK

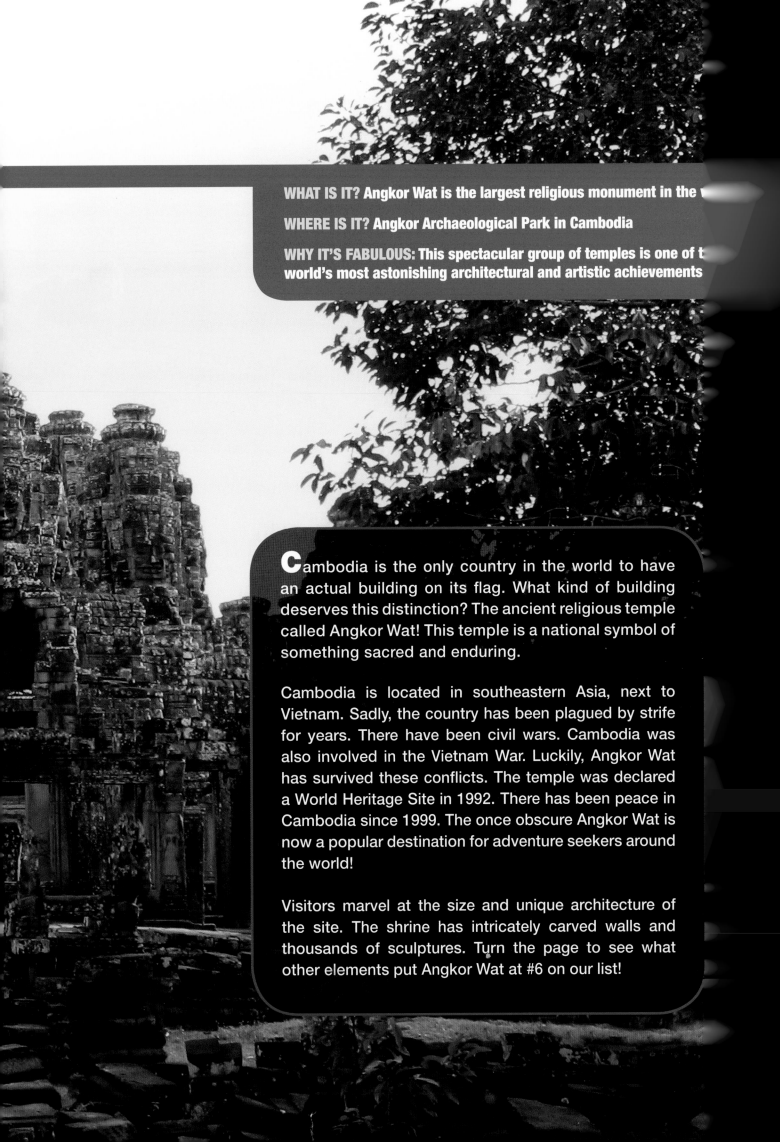

WHAT IS IT? Angkor Wat is the largest religious monument in the

WHERE IS IT? Angkor Archaeological Park in Cambodia

WHY IT'S FABULOUS: This spectacular group of temples is one of t world's most astonishing architectural and artistic achievements

Cambodia is the only country in the world to have an actual building on its flag. What kind of building deserves this distinction? The ancient religious temple called Angkor Wat! This temple is a national symbol of something sacred and enduring.

Cambodia is located in southeastern Asia, next to Vietnam. Sadly, the country has been plagued by strife for years. There have been civil wars. Cambodia was also involved in the Vietnam War. Luckily, Angkor Wat has survived these conflicts. The temple was declared a World Heritage Site in 1992. There has been peace in Cambodia since 1999. The once obscure Angkor Wat is now a popular destination for adventure seekers around the world!

Visitors marvel at the size and unique architecture of the site. The shrine has intricately carved walls and thousands of sculptures. Turn the page to see what other elements put Angkor Wat at #6 on our list!

ANGKOR WAT

ORIGINS

The temples surrounding Angkor Wat were built between the 8th and 13th centuries during the Khmer Empire. This was the largest empire of Southeast Asia. It covered parts of modern-day Vietnam, Cambodia, Laos, Thailand, and Malaysia. This powerful empire was known for its impressive architecture and art. In the 12th century, King Suryavarman II (saw-ree-yah-var-man) chose Angkor as the capital city for his empire. He built Angkor Wat as his state temple.

DETAILS

Angkor Wat is a prime example of Khmer architecture. Intricate sculptures carved into walls, entranceways guarded by long bridges, inner courtyards, and moats are just a few common elements of this style. Angkor Wat is built of sandstone and consists of a tall central cone bordered by four shorter cones. Bayon Temple is also in the Angkor Archaeological Park, which covers 154 square miles. Bayon Temple still has 37 of its original towers. Each one is decorated with gigantic sculptures of faces!

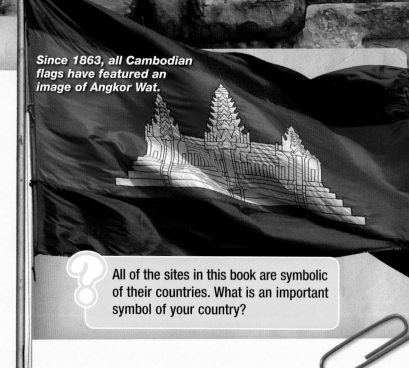

Since 1863, all Cambodian flags have featured an image of Angkor Wat.

? All of the sites in this book are symbolic of their countries. What is an important symbol of your country?

HUMAN CONNECTION

Angkor Wat was originally built as a Hindu temple. It became a Buddhist place of worship during the reign of Jayavarman VII (jie-av-are-man) at the end of the 12th century. The temples were deserted after the fall of the Khmer Empire around 1430. After this, the site was essentially "lost" for centuries. Locals talked about it, but it remained hidden by the dense, tropical jungle. In 1860, a French explorer called Henri Mouhot (moo-ho) rediscovered the ancient site.

Quick Fact

Bas-relief is shallow carving on a piece of stone or metal. The outer gallery of the Angkor Wat temple features the longest continuous bas-relief in the world!

The Expert Says...

" The volume of stone [at] the Angkor site is equal to that of the Great Pyramid of Cheops [Giza] but … the majority of it has been carved in exquisite detail. "

— Scott Murray, journalist and travel writer, *The Wonders of Angkor Wat*

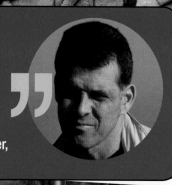

Bas-relief carving of the Khmer army

VISITORS' JOURNALS

ANGKOR WAT HAS IMPRESSED PEOPLE SINCE IT WAS FIRST BUILT. READ THESE QUOTATIONS FROM VISITORS TO THE SITE.

"It is grander than anything left to us by Greece or Rome."

— Henri Mouhot, French explorer who rediscovered Angkor Wat in 1860

"[The temple] is of such extraordinary construction that it is not possible to describe it with a pen, particularly since it is like no other building in the world. It has towers and decoration and all the *refinements* which the human genius can conceive of."

— Antonio da Magdalena, Portuguese monk who visited Angkor Wat in 1586

refinements: qualities of excellence

"[At] daybreak ... watch the temple come to life. In so doing, you will also experience the awesome solitude and reverence that only a place like Angkor can inspire."

— Scott Murray, travel writer who visited Angkor Wat in 2000

Take Note

Our #6 choice, Angkor Wat, and its surroundings tell stories about the Khmer Empire. By studying the architecture and construction of the temple, experts have also learned about building techniques and materials used in 12th century Cambodia. The fact that the temple remained hidden in a lush jungle for years only adds to its exotic appeal.

• Of the destinations you've read about so far, which one has a similar "discovery" story? Compare the two destinations under the headings following: Age, Purpose, Special Features, National Significance, and World Significance.

5   4   3   2   1

Scientific evidence shows that humans were working on the Stonehenge site as early as 3000 B.C.

WHAT IS IT? Stonehenge is a mysterious group of stones.

WHERE IS IT? Salisbury Plain, 85 miles southwest of London, England

WHY IT'S FABULOUS: Archeologists still have no idea how the primitive people of the Bronze Age were able to build this monument. Some of Stonehenge's largest stones weigh as much as 25 SUVs each!

Imagine the blood, sweat, and tears that went into the construction of Stonehenge …

Some of its stones weigh 55 tons each and were dragged from a site 18 miles to the south. Other 5.5-ton stones came from mountains nearly 240 miles away.

Building blocks this huge would be overwhelming even with modern technology. When construction started, this crew did not have bulldozers, backhoes, or cranes. They had ropes, wooden levers, and primitive tools made of stone or deer antlers.

Archeologists say that Stonehenge took over 2,000 years to build and that 25 generations of people were involved with its construction. How did they do it? Why did they do it? Amazingly, in over 5,000 years, no one has ever figured out those answers. Some experts think that Stonehenge was an astronomer's tool, part of an ancient calendar, or a temple to the sun. This is because at certain times of the year, the sun's light shines directly through to the center of the structure and illuminates the Altar Stone, the structure's main stone.

Whatever its original purpose, Stonehenge was especially important to the people who created it. The mystic circles must have been the ultimate expression of the beliefs that held their society together for those two centuries. The people who built Stonehenge have given us a most enduring monument of human creativity and persistence!

STONEHENGE

ORIGINS

Stonehenge was built in three phases from around 3000 B.C. to 1600 B.C. Primitive tools that dated to 3100 B.C. have also been found at the site. Bone fragments from around 2800 B.C. indicate the second wave of building (maybe Stonehenge was Britain's earliest cemetery). The stones we see today were introduced in six stages during the third building era from 2600 to 1600 B.C. Roman coins and pottery tell us that Stonehenge was used until around 7 A.D.

DETAILS

Visitors today see only half of the initial complex. The original structure consisted of 30 upright stones set in a circle around a horseshoe. Inside the horseshoe was a smaller horseshoe of bluestones. These stones came from Wales and have a bluish tint when wet. Sixty other bluestones stood between the large horseshoe and the circle. The "Avenue" extended from the open horseshoe. A 40-ton "Heel Stone" still stands along this laneway.

The stone monuments of the third phase had much better staying power than the wooden monuments used in the second phase. The third phase was built during the Bronze Age. This period linked the Stone Age and the Iron Age and lasted from 2000 to 650 B.C. It marked the time when people began using bronze tools.

HUMAN CONNECTION

Over the years, people and the environment have caused damage to this monument. Today, there is a highway running alongside Stonehenge. Many people are worried that the highway is too close to the historic monument. Some have suggested building a tunnel for traffic. Today only Druids, people who practice the ancient Celtic religion of Druidry, are allowed to enter the inner circle at Stonehenge. Druids worship elements in nature, like the sun and moon. Because of Stonehenge's alignment with the sun, the structure has important significance for Druids. Druids enter the inner circle to celebrate the yearly solstices.

---

solstices: *two times in the year when the sun is farthest away from the equator*

? Do you think the British taxpayers should have to pay for the new tunnel? Why or why not?

Druids celebrate the yearly solstices in Stonehenge's inner circle.

Quick Fact

In 2007, archeologists found a prehistoric village near Stonehenge. They think the people who built the third phase of Stonehenge lived there. Why they wanted to live near this specific site, and build a monument here, is still a mystery.

A model of how Stonehenge may have originally looked

The Expert Says...

"Some of the stones were brought from a long way away ... which [shows] how important that spot on Salisbury Plain must be if they went to all that trouble to get those stones to that particular place."

— Christopher Witcombe, professor and authority on Stonehenge

10   9   8   7   6

ONCE UPON A TIME...

Stonehenge remains one of the world's greatest mysteries. People have used everything from mythical stories to wacky experiments to try to explain the inexplicable. Read these anecdotes and see what you think!

Every year, close to a million people visit Stonehenge.

MYTH
"HEEL STONE" FOLKTALE

A demon bought magical stones and levitated them to Salisbury Plain. He dared the villagers to count the stones. According to legend, this was impossible. The town friar, knowing this, said there were "too many to tell." The bad-tempered demon angrily threw a stone, striking the friar in the heel but leaving him unhurt. The stone was dented and stuck in the ground! Ever since then, it's been called the "Heel Stone."

MERLIN THE MAGICIAN

King Aurelius Ambrosius wanted to build a monument on Salisbury Plain, the gravesite of Saxon soldiers. He asked Merlin the Magician where to find the proper stones for such a monument. Merlin recommended the "Giant's Dance," a circle of stones on an Irish mountain. These stones had miraculous healing power and were supposedly brought from Africa to Ireland long before by giants. After locating the stones, Aurelius's army couldn't budge them. Merlin came to the rescue and magically moved them to Salisbury, where he built Stonehenge.

REALITY
REENACTMENT

In a 2001 experiment, archeologists transported a similar stone to those used in Stonehenge along a land-sea route from Wales. With great difficulty, volunteers pulled it for a long distance on a wooden sled using the advantage of smooth modern roads and sliding nets. Then, they moved it onto a replica of an ancient boat. The boat sank!

Take Note

Stonehenge is the oldest site on our list. We still don't know how people could have moved such heavy stones and built such a perfectly circular structure. For the mystery surrounding it, the age of the site, and the important historical lessons it teaches, we've ranked it #5.
• In what ways is Stonehenge similar to Angkor Wat at #6?

5   4   3   2   1

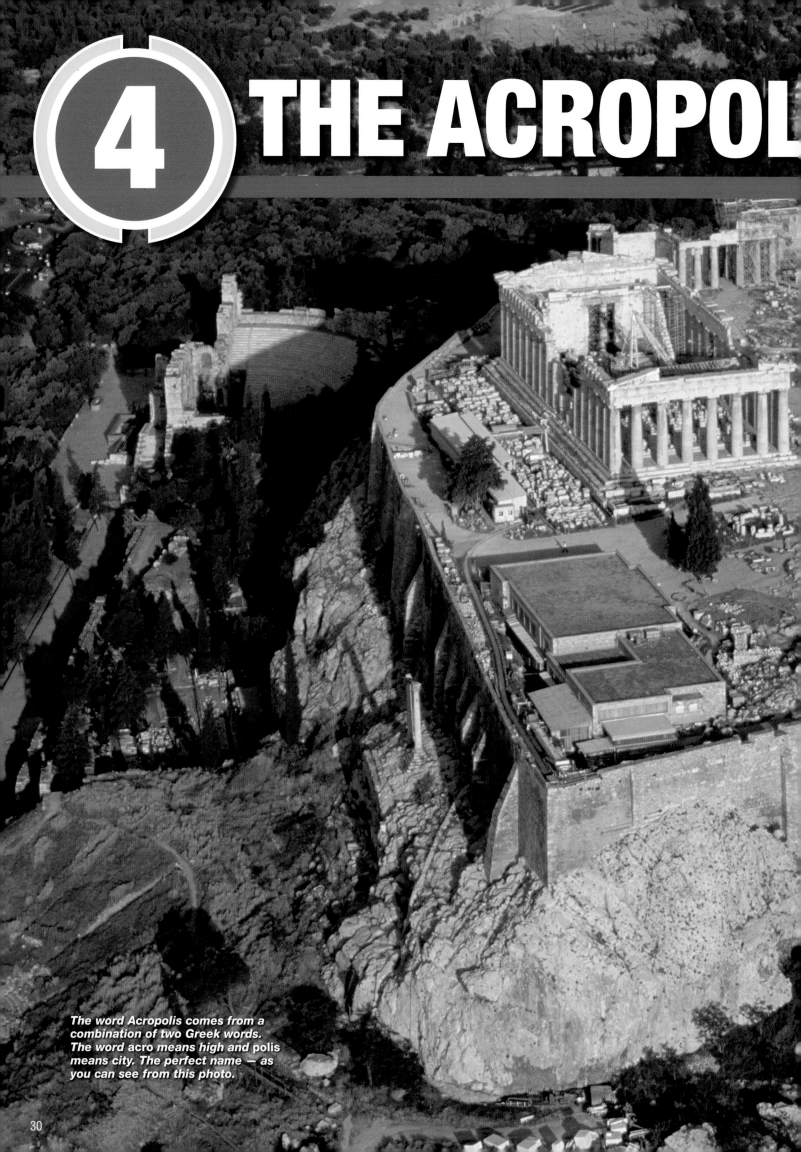

The word Acropolis comes from a combination of two Greek words. The word *acro* means high and *polis* means city. The perfect name — as you can see from this photo.

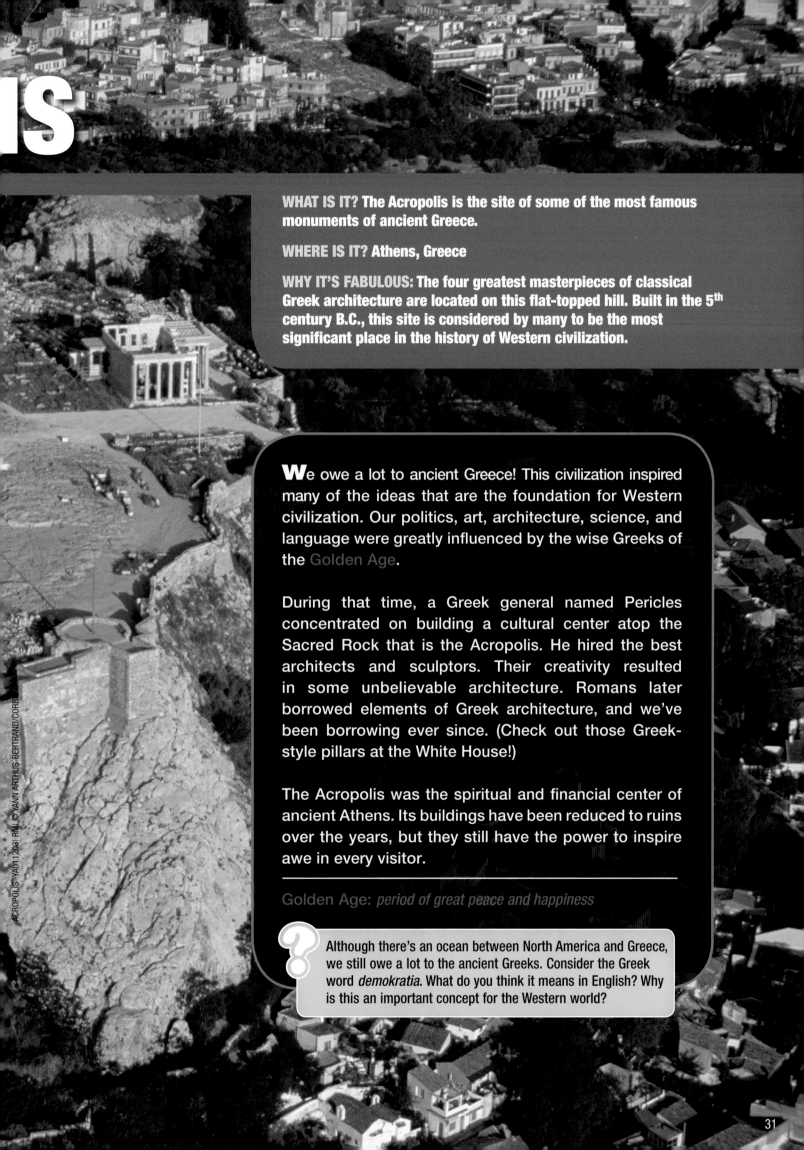

WHAT IS IT? The Acropolis is the site of some of the most famous monuments of ancient Greece.

WHERE IS IT? Athens, Greece

WHY IT'S FABULOUS: The four greatest masterpieces of classical Greek architecture are located on this flat-topped hill. Built in the 5th century B.C., this site is considered by many to be the most significant place in the history of Western civilization.

We owe a lot to ancient Greece! This civilization inspired many of the ideas that are the foundation for Western civilization. Our politics, art, architecture, science, and language were greatly influenced by the wise Greeks of the Golden Age.

During that time, a Greek general named Pericles concentrated on building a cultural center atop the Sacred Rock that is the Acropolis. He hired the best architects and sculptors. Their creativity resulted in some unbelievable architecture. Romans later borrowed elements of Greek architecture, and we've been borrowing ever since. (Check out those Greek-style pillars at the White House!)

The Acropolis was the spiritual and financial center of ancient Athens. Its buildings have been reduced to ruins over the years, but they still have the power to inspire awe in every visitor.

Golden Age: *period of great peace and happiness*

? Although there's an ocean between North America and Greece, we still owe a lot to the ancient Greeks. Consider the Greek word *demokratia*. What do you think it means in English? Why is this an important concept for the Western world?

ACROPOLIS-YA01.12031 RM. © YANN ARTHUS-BERTRAND/CORB

THE ACROPOLIS

ORIGINS

The Acropolis was a popular locale as far back as the 13th century B.C. The Mycenaeans (my-see-nee-ahns) were the first people to construct on this high hill. Since it is the highest place in the city, this location was also the safest. Between 500 and 448 B.C., Greece was under attack from the Persian Empire, modern-day Iran. During the Persian Wars, the buildings of the Acropolis were destroyed. The famous Parthenon was the first building to be rebuilt.

DETAILS

The main entrance to the Acropolis is the impressive Propylaea (prop-uh-lee-ah). To the right of the entrance is the Temple of Athena Nike. Nike was the word for victory in ancient Greece. The Parthenon is the largest structure on the Acropolis. It is a huge temple dedicated to Athena. Another temple, the Erechtheion (er-ik-thay-uh-n), was dedicated to Athena and Poseidon, the god of the sea.

Mycenaeans: *people of the Bronze Age (1400 to 1100 B.C.) culture of the eastern Mediterranean area*

? Archeological sites consist of layers of structures and debris that provide evidence of the lifestyle of societies that resided there in the past. Why is the Acropolis such an important archeological site?

HUMAN CONNECTION

Pericles was a politician who had a great influence on Athens. The Acropolis was Pericles' amazing idea. The Age of Pericles took place in the 5th century B.C. The buildings on the Acropolis helped to give people work and to beautify the city. Athens became known for its culture during this time.

Over time, the buildings of the Acropolis have been partially destroyed. Various invaders, including Sulla, the Roman dictator who attacked Athens in 86 B.C., caused severe damage to the buildings. The Acropolis has been used as a fortress and residence. The Parthenon has gone from temple to Catholic Church to mosque and back again. Between 1453 and 1829, Greece was under Turkish rule. Turkish captors used the Parthenon to store gunpowder. In 1687, the roof was blown off when invaders from Venice, Italy, attacked.

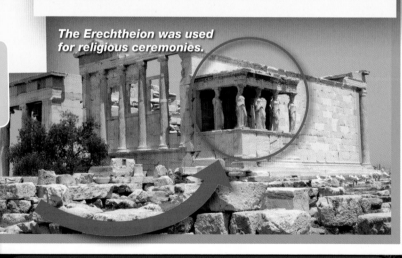

The Erechtheion was used for religious ceremonies.

Area of the Erechtheion — often called the Porch of Maidens

The Expert Says...

"[Whether] you're looking at law, architecture, show business and theater, philosophy — you can trace them back to Athens, about 500 [B.C.]."

— John Camp, archeologist

10   8   7   6

CULTURE CRADLE

Many things that are part of our everyday lives originated in ancient Greece. Read this list of Greek ideas and inventions!

NIKE — You may know it as the famous athletics company, but long before it stood for workout gear, the name Nike meant something else in ancient Greece. The word meant victory in ancient Greece and was also the name of the Greek goddess of victory and triumph. She was often portrayed sitting next to Zeus, the most important Greek god.

OLYMPICS — The first Olympic Games were held in 776 B.C. to honor the Greek god Zeus. Athletes traveled from different city-states to Athens to compete. Originally there was only one event (a run), and the games lasted only one day. Today we have summer and winter Olympics that each last over two weeks and involve thousands of athletes from around the world.

Quick Fact

According to the Nike company, the famous "swoosh" logo represents the wing of the Greek goddess.

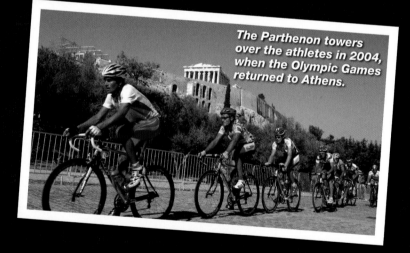

The Parthenon towers over the athletes in 2004, when the Olympic Games returned to Athens.

PHILOSOPHY — The word philosophy comes from the Greek words *philo*, meaning to love, and *sophia*, to be wise. Ancient Greeks were very interested in discovering truths and realities about life and the world. Socrates, who lived from 469 to 399 B.C., is one of the world's most famous philosophers. He explored ethics, the study of "right" and "wrong" human behavior.

Take Note

Its age, its history, and the magnificence of its architecture make the Acropolis an obvious choice for this list of ancient sites. It ranks #4 because of its significance to Western civilization. Stonehenge is very valuable for the secrets it holds, but we know a lot more about the Acropolis.
• Compare the Acropolis to another destination you have read about. What is the significance of each of them as an ancient site?

5   **4**   3   2

③ TAJ MAHAL

The Taj Mahal was built by Shah Jahan to honor his wife.

TAJ MAHAL–SHUTTERSTOCK

34

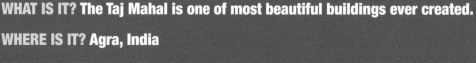

WHAT IS IT? The Taj Mahal is one of most beautiful buildings ever created.

WHERE IS IT? Agra, India

WHY IT'S FABULOUS: This tomb is not just a structure — it is a work of art. The true love it symbolizes makes it the most romantic destination.

Once upon a time, in the year 1607, there was a Mughal prince named Khurram (koor-rum). He was only 15 years old, but he was looking for a wife.

One day, he was visiting the market and caught sight of a beautiful girl selling colorful glass beads. Enchanted, he picked up a glass bead and asked her its price. She smiled and teasingly told him that it was a diamond, not glass, and that he couldn't afford it because it was 10,000 rupees. She was wrong because Khurram was a very wealthy prince. The prince learned that her name was Arjumand Banu Begum (ahr-joo-mand ba-noo bee-gum).

Khurram asked his father, Emperor Jahangir (juh-hahn-geer), for permission to marry Arjumand. His father told him that for political reasons Khurram would have to marry a Persian princess first. Since men were allowed to marry more than one wife, the emperor said Khurram could marry Arjumand afterward. Khurram married the princess but five years passed before he could make Arjumand his second wife. They finally had a grand wedding.

But that's just the beginning. What started with a glass bead ended in a beautiful jewel-encrusted building.

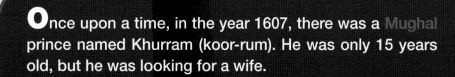

Mughal: *refers to Muslim rule in India between the 16th and 19th century*
rupees: *basic unit of money in India*

TAJ MAHAL

ORIGINS

After Emperor Jahangir's death, Khurram ascended the throne. Following custom, he was renamed Shah Jahan and Arjumand was renamed Mumtaz Mahal (moom-taz ma-hal). When she died in 1631, Shah Jahan was devastated. He decided to build the most beautiful monument in the world to honor her memory. Between 1631 and 1648, it took over 22,000 workers and 1,000 elephants to build the Taj Mahal. White marble, 40 types of gems, and other building materials were imported from China and the East.

ascended: *rose from a lower level or station; advanced to*

DETAILS

A majestic main gateway dramatically frames the Taj Mahal. A river flows behind the monument and there is an elaborate garden with four reflecting pools in the front. The complex is surrounded on three sides by a red sandstone wall. On one side there is a mosque, and a guest house stands on the other. The Taj Mahal is a white marble building, inlaid with precious stones, and topped with a massive dome.

HUMAN CONNECTION

It was common for Mughal emperors to have many wives and Shah Jahan was no exception. He had three wives and many children. Shah Jahan's youngest son, Aurangzeb (awr-uh-ng-zeb), disapproved of the amount of money his father spent on the Taj Mahal. The Emperor became ill in 1657 and his youngest son made his move. He imprisoned his father, took control from his older brothers, and became the 6th Mughal Emperor. Shah Jahan died while still under arrest. He was buried next to Mumtaz in the Taj Mahal.

This story sounds like a sad fairy tale, but it's all true. Do you think that the love story associated with the Taj Mahal adds to its appeal? Explain your answer.

Quick Fact

The Taj Mahal changes color according to different seasons and different times of day. It looks pinkish in the morning, white in the evening, and golden in the moonlight. These changes are said by locals to reflect the different moods of women.

Close to 1,000 elephants were needed to help build the Taj Mahal.

The Expert Says...

"The Taj is … a symbol of perfect love and of great beauty."

— Dr. Shobita Punja, art historian

10 9 7 6

Happily Ever After

*F*irst we told you the beginning of the love story. This descriptive account tells the rest...

Jahan and Mumtaz were happily married. Mumtaz was loved by her subjects for her kindness and beauty. She helped Jahan rule wisely and he adored her.

This couple couldn't stand to be apart from each other. Even though Mumtaz was nine months pregnant with her last child, she went with Jahan on a military trip. On a warm evening in April 1631, Mumtaz developed complications during labor.

As the legend goes, Mumtaz whispered four requests to Jahan from her deathbed. The first was that he build a beautiful monument dedicated to her. She also wanted him to remarry. The third request was for him to be kind to their children. Last of all, she asked that he visit the monument on each anniversary of her death.

As he promised, Jahan built the most beautiful monument ever created. He lived only for the Taj. In fact, he drained the country's bank account and forgot about ruling. Soon after the Taj was built, his son put Jahan in jail. From his tiny prison cell, Jahan strained to see a reflected view of the Taj. When he died, his coffin was placed beside Mumtaz's. They rest beside each other forever in a monument that is the world's ultimate symbol of enduring love.

Quick Fact

Inside and out, every wall is decorated. Much of the marble is carved. Precious gems, including diamonds, emeralds, and sapphires, were used to make flowers in the walls!

Take Note

The Taj Mahal is #3 even though it isn't as old as some of our other ancient sites. It is a symbol of ancient Indian architecture, art, and craftsmanship. Its enduring love story adds to its appeal. While the Acropolis lies in ruins, the Taj Mahal has been restored and is as beautiful today as it was when Shah Jahan finished building it in 1648.

• Should the Taj edge out the influential Acropolis? Make a list of the merits of each and decide how you would rank them.

5   4   **3**   2   1

2 GIZA PYRAMI

During the summer solstice, the sun sets in the exact center of the two largest pyramids.

We must confess that our idea of listing the 10 most wondrous ancient sites isn't original! The concept started sometime between 150 and 130 B.C. with a Greek poet named Antipater of Sidon. He gets credit for listing the seven wonders of the world in one of his poems.

Antipater named the Great Pyramid of Giza as one of those seven wonders. His other picks were the Hanging Gardens of Babylon, the Statue of Zeus at Olympia, the Temple of Artemis, the Lighthouse of Alexandria, the Colossus of Rhodes, and the Mausoleum of Halicarnassus. Even back then, the pyramids were a wondrous site. Although some theories say they are 10,000 years old, most dating attempts point to somewhere between 2589 and 2467 B.C.

And they aren't just old — they're huge. In fact, the pyramids remain among the most colossal buildings on Earth. The Great Pyramid of Giza has a base covering 568,500 square feet. It is 450 feet tall. Some of the stone blocks weigh as much as 17 tons. Not impressed? Think about the triangular design. No one is sure how the Egyptians managed to create such perfect pyramids.

Giza is the ultimate symbol of endurance and our #2 most wondrous ancient site.

GIZA PYRAMIDS

ORIGINS

During the 25th century B.C., Pharaoh Sneferu (snef-roo) built the Red Pyramid on another site. At Giza, he was outdone by his son Khufu (koo-foo) (aka Cheops), who built the largest of all existing pyramids. It is now called the Great Pyramid (or Khufu's pyramid). Khufu's son Khafre (kaf-rey) followed his father's footsteps but built a slightly smaller pyramid. Menkaure (men-ka-u-ray), Khafre's son, ended the competition with the more modest third Giza tomb.

Pharaoh: *title of an ancient Egyptian king*

Quick Fact

What's inside the Great Pyramid? There are three burial chambers. The largest is the unfinished bottom chamber. The middle, or Queen's Chamber, is the smallest. On top is the King's Chamber.

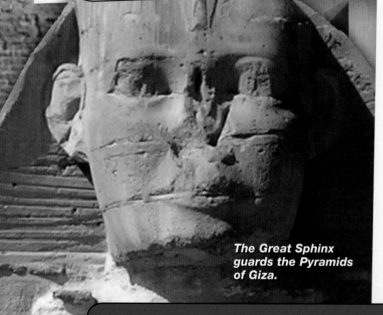

The Great Sphinx guards the Pyramids of Giza.

DETAILS

Guarding the three pyramids of Giza is the Great Sphinx. The Sphinx has the body of a lion and the head of a human. The head was probably made to look like that of Khufu. The Sphinx is one of the world's largest single-stone statues. The smaller Queens' pyramids were near the Great Pyramid. Each of the three main pyramids also had temples and graves for the royal relatives.

The stone blocks in the Great Pyramid average over two tons each and some weigh over nine tons. About 2.3 million limestone rocks were used in this structure alone!

HUMAN CONNECTION

The Old Kingdom of ancient Egypt spanned approximately 450 years between the 26th and 22nd centuries B.C. King Khufu was the fourth generation of his family to reign during the Old Kingdom. This has been called the Golden Age of Egypt. The accomplishments and cultural progress that occurred during this period give it this name.

Pharaohs created pyramids to serve as their tombs and to protect them after they died. Ancient Egyptians believed in life after death. That's why they were buried with gold, perfume, furniture — everything they might need to make the next life more comfortable. Boats were even found buried alongside the pyramids to help the pharaohs travel to the afterlife.

The Expert Says...

" I believe that we've only found about 30 percent of Egyptian monuments, that 70 percent of them still lie buried underneath the ground. "

— Dr. Zahi Hawass, archeologist and Egyptologist, Secretary General of the Supreme Council of Antiquities

Dr. Hawass was in charge of the exploration and the preservation of Giza. Recently, two more pyramids were found there beneath the sand! Why do you think it is crucial to protect this important site while examining the area?

HOW DO THE PYRAMIDS STACK UP?

CHECK OUT THESE AMAZING FACTS ABOUT THE MOST ENDURING MONUMENTS ON EARTH ...

The outer layer of the Great Pyramid (Khufu's pyramid) was made of almost 150,000 stones. Each one weighed more than 14 tons. These were made of polished white limestone. Each one was more than eight feet thick. Most of these have been stolen from the structure.

 Why is it important to learn about and respect the customs and culture of places we choose to visit?

The Great Pyramid's total mass is estimated at six million tons. People have estimated that to build the Great Pyramid in only 20 years, 1.1 blocks would have to be put in place every two minutes for 10 hours a day. This would have to be repeated every day for 20 years!

Originally, the Great Pyramid was 482 feet tall. It has eroded to about 450 feet. The Eiffel Tower is 1,050 feet tall. The Empire State Building is more than three times as tall, at 1,450 feet. The CN Tower still tops them all at more than 1,800 feet! But, none compares in volume or mass to the Great Pyramid.

Quick Fact

After the Giza complex, Egyptians continued building more modest pyramids for around 1,000 years. There are over 100 other pyramids in Egypt.

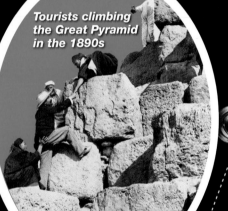

Tourists climbing the Great Pyramid in the 1890s

Total weight: six million tons!

Take Note

Scientists are still trying to understand the ancient Egyptian method of building. The pyramids are massive and some of the oldest structures still in existence. They are older than the Taj Mahal. They were also much harder to build because of their complicated design. For all these reasons and for being the icon of Egypt, the pyramids take the #2 spot.

• The Acropolis represents another Golden Age. How do these two sites compare? Which one do you think is more amazing and why?

CN Tower

Empire State Building

Eiffel Tower

The Great Pyramid

5   4   3   2   1

1 THE GREAT

The Great Wall snakes its way up and down mountain ridges through some of the most ruggedly magnificent terrain on Earth.

THE GREAT WALL-SHUTTERSTOCK

WALL

WHAT IS IT? The Great Wall is a 4,535-mile-long fortification.

WHERE IS IT? The wall runs near the northern boundary of China from a seaport on the east coast to Xinjiang (shin-jee-ah-ng) in the northwest.

WHY IT'S FABULOUS: The Great Wall took more than 2,000 years to build!

"It sure is a great wall."

Have you ever made a stupid comment and immediately wished you hadn't sounded so silly? That's probably how President Nixon felt when he made this remark about the Great Wall during his historic 1972 visit. After years of tense U.S. relations with China, Nixon was trying to warm up the relationship. There he was, the world's most powerful official at one of the world's most impressive sites, and what does he think of to say?

The Great Wall really is, well, great. So great it leaves one dumbstruck. Poor Nixon was just reacting the way most people do when they see it. The wall goes on for so many miles that it is mind-boggling.

The wall is also very old. The Chinese began building it two centuries before the Greeks started the Acropolis. More than a million people helped build it and thousands died in the process.

How does one feel walking the Great Wall, knowing that each step treads upon another century-old footstep? The Great Wall is a symbol of China's impressive and enduring culture. For this reason, as well as its age, size, and the difficulty of its construction, the Great Wall of China is our #1 most wondrous ancient site.

dumbstruck: *silenced by amazement or shock*

THE GREAT WALL

ORIGINS

Between the 7th and 3rd centuries, various pieces of wall were built. The period of time, from approximately the 5th century to the middle of the 3rd century B.C., was known as the Warring States Period. During this time, each of seven states had a separate ruler. Each one was at war with the others. The Qin State became more powerful than the others and eventually conquered them all.

DETAILS

The first sections of the wall were built before the use of bricks. They were made of packed dirt and stones. The later sections were made of more permanent materials, and some sections were even paved with marble. On average, the wall is 22 to 26 feet high and between 11 and 21 feet wide.

The Great Wall was built as a fortress. It has watchtowers, barracks, and holes for shooting arrows. Guards were posted in the watchtowers and would send smoke signals to warn of invaders. The Great Wall also served as a road across otherwise impassable terrain.

HUMAN CONNECTION

In 221 B.C., China became a unified country for the first time. The Qin dynasty began at this time. Qin Shi Huang (tseen she hwahng) became the country's first emperor. When Qin Shi Huang was emperor he decided to join the existing sections of the wall. He also ordered new sections to be built. A large part of the Great Wall was also built during the Ming dynasty. This dynasty lasted from 1368 to 1644 A.D.

Quick Fact

In 2002, archeologists found a 50-mile-long section of the wall that had been hidden under sand for hundreds of years!

A guard in traditional dress keeps watch over the Great Wall.

The Expert Says...

"Many historians now believe that the wall, or walls, were built to mark territories, similar to the way that forts were built here in the States."

— Michael Nylan, professor of Chinese history and culture expert, University of California at Berkley

10   9   8   7   6

DRAGON ROAD

The Great Wall is often compared to a giant dragon. It rises and falls over steep mountain ridges like a dragon's tail. Indeed, it certainly swallowed a lot of lives during its construction. Learn more about this amazing destination in this article.

By name, it is a wall. It did what walls are supposed to do: define territory, keep people out, and also keep them in.

It is also a road. It crosses deserts and grasslands. It makes its way over mountains and along plateaus. It allowed the people of ancient China access to otherwise unreachable parts of their land. It united a vast country.

At just over 4,350 miles, the Wall is still one of the longest highways. In comparison, the world's longest highway, the Trans-Canada, beats it at 4,860 miles. Route 20 crosses the U.S. in 3,365 miles. The big difference is that these roads were built in modern times with modern equipment and tax dollars. The Great Wall was built with the hands and blood of the people. Much of it is still standing after so many centuries. A feat of that magnitude can never be duplicated.

Imagine climbing 3,700 steps!

Quick Fact

Most people who worked on the wall were prisoners of war. They had to watch out for invaders and work in rough country with scarce food supplies. It's estimated that more than a million laborers died during construction. The wall has been called "the longest cemetery on Earth."

? Why do you think the Chinese chose to use prisoners to build the Great Wall?

Quick Fact

The Great Wall Marathon began in 1999 and several hundred racers participate each year. It's more of a challenge than usual marathons because the course includes very steep sections and 3,700 stone steps!

Take Note

The scope of the Great Wall is beyond imagination. The Wall was not built on one site, but across a massive country. Its construction kept people busy for centuries. It wasn't built for religion, burial, or entertainment — it was built for defense. The difficulty of constructing the Great Wall and the vastness of the project put it at #1.
• Many sections of the Great Wall have been vandalized. People have painted and resurfaced sections to "improve" it and attract more tourists. Do you think people living near the Great Wall think of it differently from the way we do? Explain your answer.

3   2   1

We Thought …

Here are the criteria we used in ranking the 10 most wondrous ancient sites.

The site/structure:
- Was beautifully designed
- Featured complex construction
- Was an impressive size
- Was historically and culturally significant
- Has endured for centuries
- Has unique features